D1307655

Smile

Published by MQ Publications Limited
12 The Ivories
6–8 Northampton Street
London, N1 2HY
email: mail@mqpublications.com
website: www.mqpublications.com

For inquiries about Daiensai contact:
The Kirsten Gallery,
5320 Roosevelt Way N.E.,
Seattle, WA 98105
email: kirstengallery@earthlink.net
website: www.kirstengallery.com

Design: Balley Design Associates
Editor: Laura Kesner

ISBN: 1-84072-594-X

10 9 8 7 6 5 4 3 2 1

Printed and bound in China

Smile

365 Happy Meditations

**Richard
Kirsten Daiensai**

MQP

Introduction

I was ordained a Zen priest on 26 October 1967 in Zuisenji Temple, Kamakura, Japan, and given the name Daiensai Kuden Bon Seki Dojin. Since that date, all of my artworks are signed with both my western and Zen Buddhist name, shortened to Daiensai. Every year since 1958, I have pilgrimaged to many different parts of Japan, and more recently, Korea. These journeys marked a flowing into Zen and Shinto consciousness—embracing the energy of the eastern heart, mind, and spirit.

All of the meditations and artworks in the book explore the intuitive, creative, and mystical forces that result from various levels of consciousness and trance states reached via meditations.

For 45 years, I have filled journals with meditations, art, photos, sketches, and random writings of my mystical experiences and humor. The art and writing from my journals have been pieced together in this, my first published book. I hope and pray that you will find love, joy, and peace in the meditations and artwork.

I give thanks to my family and the various masters and monks in the many temples of Japan and Korea that have befriended me over the years. Thanks must also go to the many friends and patrons that have helped me, and to everyone at MQ Publications who so lovingly worked on this book.

"Love is love, even just putting your thoughts, around each other."

Richard Kirsten Daiensai

1 | *Everything—
that will be,
is already in
the seed.*

2 | Start each day
with a smile
and
it will be
a joy
for everyone.

3 | Each unborn seed
voyages
amongst the stars
patiently
waiting to be reborn.

4 The path
leads
from star to star.

5 *Every seed
knows how
to strive
for the light.*

6 Even a seed,
in its sleep,
awaits
the light.

1 | Each new day,
a joyful song.

8 | What deities labored
at setting fire
to the sun?

9 | *All humanity*
dwells
in the howl
of a wolf.

10 | Each new day
is a rebirth,
cherish it
for it is a gift
from the gods.

11 | Only a
cloud,
knows
the feeling
of a cloud.

12 | *Listening,*
to the sacred voice
of silence.

13 | *Full moon,*
and everything
is transformed.

14 | The flowers
of spring
utter no words
yet they
emanate
the essence
of Zen.

15 | *The pine has*
no voice
but when
the wind blows
it sings.

16 | I welcome
solitude and silence,
the Mother and Father
of my creativity.

17 | *He duck—She duck,*
on a spiritual journey, of love.

18 | *Birds,*
flowers,
bones and stones,
converse,
with each other.

19 | Only the
stream,
knows,
where it is going.

20 | Even inorganic objects
are divine entities,
as are animals,
trees,
rivers,
mountains,
sun,
moon,
stars,
and Earth,
are sentient beings.

21 | One speck of dust, contains, all things.

22 | O moon
of all seasons—
moving the tides
and the mountains,
and within us,
too.

23 | Caressing the blossoms
with heart, mind, and soul,
one becomes transcendent
with the ecstasy that
embraces all seasons.

24 | Oh, yes, yes O flower,
your divine influence,
is everywhere.

25 | The white butterfly,
the black butterfly,
see how they seek
pleasure
from the same flower.

26 | *One can renounce the world,
but,
not the moon and flowers.*

27 | Let us pay homage,
to the snail,
who knows the bliss
of enjoying all of life,
slowly.

28 | Just as plants
sprout from the earth
so does everything
arise from the imperishable.

29 | We are all,
like a passing wave,
in the sea
of eternity.

30 | *Be happy
all life,
some sun,
some rain.*

31 | Forget yourself
and become
the universe.

32 | *Ecstasy,*
dwells in the universe,
of enlightenment.

33 | What we become
is what we think,
all that we are
arises with
our thoughts,
it is we that create
the world and the universe.
(Buddha)

34 | The true sage
laughs,
at the universe,
and
the universe,
laughs back.

35 | In the greed
for the fruit,
one misses the flowers.

36 Gratitude swimming in the spring sky.

37 | Dearly beloved,
in the drifting mists of time,
nature of humanity,
the very existence of love,
life, art, and poetry
exists and emanates,
from a single flower.

38 | The flower,
that only blooms for a day,
never forgets
the sunrise.

39 | *Even when they*
bloom,
some
never see
the flowers.

40 | A major flower?
a minor flower?
is there such a thing?
flower is flower.

41| The seeds,
that come
to Earth,
exist also
in other universes.

42| Positive, or negative,
the seeds,
are in you.

43 | Growth—
the roots are you,
the leaves
are your learning,
the flower
is your love and understanding,
the seeds
are what you give,
to others.

44 | *Produce blossoms,*
and the fruit,
if you want
understanding,
from others.

45 | *Tending one's garden,*
one becomes one,
with the universe.

46 | We are
in the garden,
let us open our eyes.

47 | *In everything,*
there is,
a communication
of spirit.

48 | Flower of purity,
flower of desire,
each
emanating a silent sermon.

49 | Hearing
the petals fall,
the sleeper,
is awakened.

50 | Each season
of life,
has its own flowers,
its own weeds.

51 | *When pulling weeds,*
pull,
all your own
first.

52 | If,
you cut away
the root,
nothing grows.

53 | Young sage,
listening, to the advice
of a crow.

54 | *What is the name*
of that bird?
does it matter?
bird is bird.

55 | No bird can fly
in two directions
at once.

56 | Knowledge
studies others,
wisdom
is self known.

57 | The bird of Zen—
is the crow.

58 | *Crow,*
seeking the advice,
of
a master.

59 | *A great teacher,*
always,
in all ways,
remains
a student.

60 | A master
can open doors
for you
but
you need to enter.

61 The sage,
sees without seeing,
and does his works
without doing.

62 *Silence and solitude,*
strengthens, the divine spirit,
reflected thru love,
work, and deeds.

63 | We live and die
and dream, on and on,
in an endless cosmos
of a billion suns,
plenty of space
for all
rebirths.

64 | *Let us merge,*
into the heartbeat,
of all things.

65 | Even before
the beginning,
cosmic Mind,
was there.

66 | Zen mind is still,
quiet,
tranquil,
and yet always moving
and seeking.

67 | Fish seeking advice
on the possibility of becoming
human in his next life.

68 | If
there is
sincerity of heart and mind,
even without prayers,
the gods will provide protection.

69 | Please understand
that your outer life,
reflects,
your inner heart
and mind.

70 | *The divine*
isn't only God,
it's all things.

71 There is no village
where the moon
doesn't shine.

72 | Rain is from God,
acid rain,
is from man.

73 Emanate
love,
joy,
and happiness
as best you can,
for most of humanity
is unhappy enough.

74 Learn
to bless,
things and people,
and everything that touche
your life.

75 | Sharing,
whatever you have,
is one
of life's joys.

Give thanks,
for the simple things
in our life.

77 | At the time of the full moon,
a fisherman's wife's offering, of gratitude,
to the gods of the sea.

78 | *Moon, entering,*
a Zen garden.

79 | Stone Buddha image,
happy, to become
a bird perch.

80 Our true home,
it's in the present
moment.

81 This old, old, old
pine tree
dreaming, dreaming, dreaming.

82 | All
the streams and rivers
continue to flow,
to the ocean,
cosmic consciousness,
receives them all.

83 | The beautiful snowflake,
disappears,
amongst
the snowflakes.

84 *One*
who sees all beings
within the self,
and the self,
within
all beings,
is enlightened.

85 Possessions,
all of them,
are impermanent,
true understanding cannot be found
in the material
world.

86 Even in a speck,
of dust,
there is,
the Buddha Nature.

87 The God you touch,
is the God,
that touches
you.

88 One
can change their life,
only as much
as one is willing.

89 | Everyone
goes through the meadow,
but only few
see the flowers.

90 | *Through your meditations,*
your life,
will have more meaning.

91 | Treasure
that blessed gift,
your life.

92 | *The flower*
of spiritual faith
has no thorns
of doubt.

93 | The voice,
of a wayside flower,
doesn't attract a busy mind.

94 | All flowers,
emanate, their
Buddha Nature.

95 Be at peace
within yourself
and you will emanate
peace to others.

96 The greedy
never know
the true meaning
of inner peace.

97 | *Listening,*
from the heart,
beats,
listening from the mind.

98 | Only
when knowledge and
experience,
enters the heart,
does it become wisdom.

99 *Before*
the universe was
formed,
Mind was there.

100 With one stroke
of the brush,
forget
all that you know.

101 | *The heart,*
is the gate,
to all Buddhas.

102 | The value
of all life
is equal.

103 | Ancient sage,
listening, to the conversation
between the flower and the stone.

104 | Seeing,
with only the physical eyes,
borders on blindness.

105 | *Already a Buddha*
ages ago,
the old pine tree,
dreaming,
dreaming.

106 | Never forget,
Yin and Yang,
is a universal law.

107 | Zen laugh,
knowing,
that what is important
is not important.

108 | *Courage,*
is the strength
to be different, from the crowd

109 | Breathing in,
I smile,
breathing out,
I smile,
thinking with my heart
enjoying this moment.

110 Ecstasy,
opens the door,
to transformations.

111 *Take time
to laugh,
for it is the music,
of the soul.*

112 | To respect
life,
every day in every way,
is enlightenment.

113 | Know the value
of silence and solitude,
they have many gifts
to share with you.

114 | *There is*
a light, within,
the heart-mind,
called
self-illumination.

115 | *The state of the heart and mind,*
cannot be known,
by most of humanity.

116 | Sometimes,
the dream chases reality,
sometimes, reality chases the dream,
and dream chases dream,
sometimes.

117 | *Not in the*
garden of the mind,
but in the
garden of the heart—
bloom the flowers
of love and understanding.

118 There is
no peace of mind,
without
peace of heart.

119 *Where does thought,*
your thought
come from?
is it from your mind
or
is it from your heart?
meditate
on the difference.

120 Finding
your quiet mind,
opens up
the joy,
of inner peace.

121 A moment in eternity
eternity in a moment—
meditation.

122 | Be happy,
while
awaiting,
happiness.

123 | Using your imagination,
even a stone,
can grow
hair.

124 | *Stones—*
some are awake and meditate,
while others
sleep.

125 | *The divine*
comedy
of being.

126 | The veneration of two stones,
nestling together,
with love.

127 No sense of time
or place,
round or square,
up or down,
no north,
south,
east or west,
only an awakening,
of the bliss
of love.

128 *Love
is love,
even just putting your thought
around each other.*

129 *Let all
that you do,
be done
with love.*

130 Let your heart,
sing,
of harmony and love.

131 | Some things
cannot be taught,
but are passed
from heart
to heart,
without words.

132 | Love,
is something
that nobody,
likes cold.

133 | *If*
we did not do
as we do,
I would not be me,
nor
would you,
be you.

134 | Star filled night sky,
everything,
is filled with eternity,
your hand in mine.

135 | All lovers are star gazers.

136 | *There is*
a divine music,
that is
only heard,
by lovers.

137 | *A flute,*
without a hole,
makes no music.

138 | The light of love
and compassion
is eternal.

139 | There is a talent—
beyond talent,
a gift beyond gifts,
it is the art of love,
and the ability, to express
the divine,
that dwells in all things.

140 | *Your happiness, is my happiness.*

141 Life
may be short
but
love and a smile
will carry you through
all your life.

142 *Our soul,*
in all our dreams,
is free.

143 | However
fleeting joy is,
joy is joy.

144 | Love,
it awakens transcendental
spiritual awakening.

145 | *Kindness and gratitu*
is the path,
of love.

146 | The words
that dwell in my heart,
are,
I love you all.

147 | There is hard
in the soft
and soft
in the hard.

148 | Whosoever, lives
contented with little,
possesses everything,
inner peace.

149 | Both,
the dark
and the light,
arouse each other.

150 | New moon,
stars,
an offering of flowers
to six stone saints,
joyous,
in the ecstasy
of love.

151 *Love,*
can warm,
even,
the coldest heart.

152 Without desire,
nothing, is accomplished.

153 | Make love
the sun in your life,
without it,
we grow old
before our time.

154 | The rising smoke
of incense,
it writes the sutra,
of everlasting love.

155 | All lovers,
become,
the ecstasy of the stream
as it enters the sea.

156 | *Anger, only exists,*
where there is
lack, of love.

157 | The three virtues,
meditate upon them,
faith, love, and hope.

158 | If,
you cannot love,
you will never know,
peace.

159 | *There is no such thing, as too many, hugs.*

160 | *Humor,
it's necessary
for survival.*

161 | Love, life, desire,
is a pure flame
within us
fed by an invisible sun
called
the divine spirit.

162 | A kiss,
is no kiss,
without love.

163 | The love,
of silence and solitude,
is the awakening,
of wisdom.

164 | O little child,
formed,
from love and devotion,
grow
in heart and spirit,
and
pass on love,
to everyone.

165 | *A home,*
should be
like entering, the hear
of a dove.

166 | Turn your heart and mind inward
and you will
find your pathway.

167 | Every thought,
moves,
into the next thought—
move slowly.

168 | The silence,
between songs,
is, also a song.

169 | When the mind,
is quiet,
the heart listens.

170 | If,
you cannot
love unconditionally,
you, will never know
peace.

171 | For the unconditional love
that a pet gives to us,
we give thanks.

172 | *A smiling heart,*
will,
bring good fortune.

173 | Hate,
only exists,
where there is
an absence,
of love.

174 | *If you can smile,*
at
the faults of yourself,
you,
can smile,
at
the faults of others.

175 | Don't wait,
to show your love,
by kissing the tombstone.

176 | The whole destiny
of human existence
is to awaken
the light of love and peace
from the darkness
of mere being.

177 | *Ecstasy—*
is sometimes hidden,
but always present,
nobody knows
who gave it birth,
but it is older than old,
and here to stay.

178 | W-O-R-K
can be spelled
J-O-Y,
if you love what it is,
that you do.

179 Do things
for others,
without expecting, any reward.

180 *Fame,*
is like the smoke
of incense,
sweet smelling as it is,
it fades to nothing.

181 | Let all that you do,
be done,
with love.

182 | All evil
comes
from a lack
of unconditional love.

183 | O Lord Buddha,
we all know,
to touch,
with love,
is healing.

184 | *You,*
cannot change the world,
but,
you can change yourself.

185 | Be a student
all life long.

186 | We must voyage beyond intellect.

187 | *Without one's thoughts, the thinker, doesn't exist.*

188 | *Giving thanks to blessings, increases blessings.*

189 | When the pupil
is ready,
the teacher,
will appear.

190 | *Love too,*
an endless mystery.

191 *We are all born,*
from love—love—love—
to love.

192 The world
of reality
is but a shadow.

193 A wave of love,
can wash away,
a footprint of hatred.

194 | It is fate,
that brings two people together,
but,
it is love,
that keeps them,
together.

195 If
we meditate
together
let us reach the peak
together.

196 | If,
you do not have
peace,
in your heart,
you,
cannot
give, peace,
to anyone else.

197 | A true teacher,
remains a
student,
at all times.

198 | Possession is an illusion.

199 | It is the ego,
that can create,
unhappiness.

200 | *Break through,
the world of illusion,
meditate.*

201| Enjoy, enjoy,
for life is given
to us, only,
moment by moment.

LOVE ♥ HEALS

KIRSTEN DAIENSAI

202 The kiss,
of love,
it dwells,
in all of eternity.

203 *The everlasting peace*
comes when loved ones
are together.

204 A snake's child
is precious
to the snake.

205 Meditate,
where is
your true home?

206 One way
or another
love
shares the same
pillow.

207 Be happy,
worry, will make you sick.

208 | If you are wanting
people's approval for what you are doing
with your life,
you are their prisoner.

209 | Today,
never knows,
tomorrow.

210 | Knowledge,
that moves from the head,
into the heart,
becomes wisdom.

211 | *We all pass*
like day into night,
and lo!
from night into day,
let us celebrate.

212 | *What is certain, is that nothing is certain.*

213 | If you don't become lost, you will never be found.

214 | You—
yes you,
you cannot make anything
happen,
happen just happens.

215 | *Thank the light,*
in which,
darkness, doesn't exist.

216 | *In every winter's heart,
there is the seed, of spring.*

217 *Give us this day*
our daily dreams.

218 If you worry
about living,
you,
forget how to live.

219 | The cosmos
is a computer,
divine brain.

220 | O silence,
O solitude,
great powers you have
given me
from the sacred
void.

221 It is desire,
that takes us,
on the path
we choose.

222 *Nothing
will bring you peace
except yourself.*

223 | Who is rich?
whoever
rejoices in their portion.

224 | Before we awake,
who knows,
that
the dream,
we are dreaming
is not real?

225 | Square,
dreaming of becoming,
a circle.

226 The realization,
of not knowing,
is the first act,
of wisdom.

227 Veneration,
it awakens
things that were asleep
or forgotten.

228 *Even for a dream,*
you,
are needed.

229 | It's impossible
to bring joy
to those that relish
misery.

230 | Happy, are they,
that do not lose,
a childlike heart.

231 | *Enlightenment, comes,*
in many forms.

232 Some light,
comes,
from the crack
under the door.

233 We,
are all swimmers,
in the ocean, of dreams.

234 | *What lies before us is a small matter, compared, to what lies within us.*

235 | An optimist takes a chance at losing, a pessimist loses a chance at winning.

236 | *Come in,*
come in,
silence and solitude,
you have much,
to tell me.

237 | Meditation—
opens the secret
of existence.

238 | If you do not understand
yourself
where will you go
to get it.

239 | When you find wisdom,
you will know,
its been within you,
all the time.

240 | Being happy as a nobody
is
the secret of success.

241 | *When we enter
the world,
karma,
is born with us.*

242 | Take time
to listen,
to your inner voice.

243 | *Spirit
is beyond
destruction.*

244 | The world
of reality
is but a shadow.

245 | Two flowers,
voyaging,
in a mystic landscape.

246 | Most troubles,
are only,
a small passing storm.

247 Although the song,
in the heart
is silent,
it is reflected
in the face.

248 *There are
a series
of masks,
even
on one face.*

249 The eyes
you were born with,
see,
only the external world,
the third eye
is single,
but sees the invisible.

250 Lament not
what is,
is
and always will be.

251 Be
content, with,
what you were born with

252 *Peace of heart*
is
the goal
realized.

253 One thought
contains
3000 thoughts.

254 All,
is heart and mind
in spring,
summer, and fall too,
there is spring
and winter too
in the mind
spring.

255 *Many flee a serpent
and
meet a dragon.*

256 | *The golden cloud,*
go not outside to search,
return
into the self,
for truth dwells
in the inward person.

257 | *Speech is the waves of the ocean of thought.*

258 | All humanity—
is stuff which
all dreams
are made of.

259 | *A team
of 12 horses
cannot overtake
a word
once it is spoken.*

260 | Turn your gaze inward
and see
the divine self
within.

261 | Respect
your ancestors,
they
are a good part
of you.

262 If you didn't know,
when,
you were born,
how old would you be?

263 Eternity
is in the face of every child,
born
from the seeds,
that traveled from light,
and merged with the flesh,
reborn on Earth,
and other earths,
in the cosmos.

264 *Who you are,*
is a result
of many lives.

265 | Every family,
in every home,
each,
has their own
universe.

266 | Inside God
dwells the cosmos,
the all of everything,
and,
the all of nothing.

267 | Bird singing flowers, while awaiting, spring.

268 | *I am the circle*
of eternal flame,
self fed
from this fire,
all things proceed
in it, all things have
their being,
and to it
all things return.

269 | *Remember,*
with the first born,
the mother
is also born.

270 | Dream,
awaken,
dream,
awaken,
awaken,
dream,
awaken,
and yet,
all
is dream.

271 | *Both the coming and the going,*
a pilgrimage.

272 | Birth,
the marriage
of life and death.

273 | Let not your mind
be disturbed,
wherever you travel
there will be wind,
waves, and storm.

274 | Life,
it's like a spring snow, that falls upon a
swiftly moving stream.

275 | Fate and destiny,
cannot,
be moved by pity.

276 | Your entire future,
is determined,
by how you live your life,
today.

277 | *Wisdom,*
give the gift
of inner peace
and also longevity.

278 | If
you abandon your spirit
to please others
you will lose everything.

279 | *Fish and bird,*
discussing,
a former existence.

280 From delight
all things are born,
by delight
they exist and grow,
and to delight
they return
and are born again.

281 *The old,*
passes,
so the new
can come.

282 | *Everyone—*
returns to their source,
whatever,
their belief.

283 | The state of mind
at the time
of your death
determines
your future life.

284 | Even,
a cleaning rag,
has emotions.

285 | The path from ignorance
to enlightenment,
consumes,
many lifetimes.

286 | *The end of autumn,*
is in the color
of the last leaf.

287 | Even
pots and pans,
have their own,
enlightenment.

288 | What
is matter?
never mind,
what
is mind?
never matter.

289 | Mystic priest
carrying offerings,
to all of humanity,
gifts,
from the ancient gods and goddesses

290 Seek harmony
with others,
for we all,
share,
the same, destiny.

291 *The only path,*
to inner peace,
is not through the mind,
but,
through the heart.

292 | Visionary intuition,
leads us,
into the divine light.

293 | O spiritual travelers
beyond
ancient memories,
pursuing dreams
that are eternal.

294 | The thinker's mind,
mirrors,
a universe,
which
in turn,
mirrors, the thinker's mind

295 | Meditation,
a pilgrimage,
to the temple, of one's own bein·

296 In all universes,
and all
eternities, where have you traveled,
O mind?

297 *Whosoever,*
is born
from the womb,
knows
only this world,
whosoever,
is born
out of themselves,
sees,
other worlds.

298 | *In gratitude,
an offering, to the
autumn moon.*

299 | *How beautiful,*
the sermon,
of silence.

300 | Be joyful,
for joy
lets in light,
togetherness,
the joy
of existence.

301 *Even in winter,*
meditate,
on spring.

302 Do not
choose
a closed mind.

303 The belly laugh,
is a form of self-healing,
purification,
it brings you closer
to both,
the God of Heaven,
and
the God, of Earth.

304 Lifeha
deathha
joyha
sadha
mamaha
papaha
youha
weha
theyha
come to think of
it
all is ha ha.

305 *Wanting,*
gets in the way,
of enjoying,
what you have.

306 Joy and sorrow,
see,
how they walk,
hand in hand.

307 Spring,
is hidden,
in all seasons.

308 Were all of humanity
never to know,
sadness,
there would be
no joy.

309 Although
this life,
is only a dream,
oh—how delightful.

310 What is bliss?
it is
inner peace.

311 | *Whatever happens*
will happen,
so smile,
and don't worry,
your fate
can be seen,
in a single bone.

312 | The other shore,
ha!
it's this shore.

313 | "It's never too late,
to celebrate,"
said the dancing rabbits.

314 | The wise meditator,
leaves,
negative thoughts, behin[d]

315 | May my art
and my meditations
find a place
in your heart and soul
for they come
from my heart and soul.

316 | *Through meditation, we, all become, voyagers.*

317 | Free of attachment
to objects
and enveloped
in the heart,
the mind is no longer
the mind,
let all
become quiet
in the heart—
this is the goal
of meditation.

318 | *Patience is bitter,*
but,
bears sweet fruit.

319 | It will pass,
whatever,
it may be.

320 | If,
you earnestly persevere,
nothing,
is difficult.

321 | Is,
was, and shall be,
are time's
only children.

322 | The center
of the universe
is where you stand.

323 | *"O soul*
of the universe,
what is more important,
than knowledge?"
"caring,
and seeing,
with the heart,"
said the soul.

324 | All that is conscious
in this universe
and all universes
is absolute consciousness,
you are consciousness,
meditate
on the world
as consciousness.

325 | Thinking
with the heart
beats
thinking with the mind

326 | Never forget—
at the lowest ebb,
is the turn,
of the tide.

327 | *After
a night's sleep
in oblivion,
to awaken
in a new day
is
God's gift.*

328 | *Bird ship,*
carrying an offering, of flowers,
in the ocean of memories.

329 | *Here today,*
gone tomorrow,
back again
some way,
or another.

330 | There is no death,
only an exchange
of worlds.

331 Do not
look
at the faults
of others,
look
at yourself,
what you have done
or left undone.

332 Don't let your mind,
become,
a wastepaper basket,
that accepts
all trivia.

333 | It is action,
that gives voice, to the bell.

334 | The temple bell
is being,
the hollow center
is non-being,
neither can function.
without
the other.

335 | *All the shadows,*
in the universe,
cannot,
put out the light,
of a single candle.

336 | Doing good
every day,
in every way,
one grows old
beautifully.

337 | "All Heaven is made of birdseed," said the bird to the deer.

338 | Love,
love,
love,
and grow
younger,
as you grow
older.

339 | *The day will dawn*
for you,
when,
you, yourself
will laugh at life.

340 | *To explain the unknown—through, the known is impossible.*

341 | Ha!
what is it
that you have
that will not decay
and
pass away?

342 *Happiness,*
is the ability,
to accept one's fate.

343 You never realize
how rich you really are
until
you lose what you have.

344 | *The past and the
future
does not
exist.*

345 | Past, present, and future,
is all dream stuff.

346 | The doorway is mute,
yet speaks
eternal mystery,
timeless temptations
this life,
and
all lives to come.

347 | *Conform to the low*
and
conform to the high.

348 | Remember,
to give thanks,
to all your ancestors.

349 | It is true,
we all reap,
what we sow.

350 | The quest,
will be forgotten,
when the goal,
is reached.

351| We, all
pass,
over the bridge.

352 | All paths,
may be varied,
but,
the goal
is the same.

353 | *Even an old glove,*
seeks,
the warmth, of fingers

354 | To know the past,
is to know,
the future.

355 | Yea Heaven,
yea Earth,
I am
both of you.

356 | Wisdom,
is not the same,
as knowledge.

357 | An honest laugh
is always healing,
all ways.

358 Is paradise in the west,
or east?
or north or south?—
you can only find it
within yourself.

359 *Heaven and*
Earth,
cannot,
be separated.

360 | *The bridge of Heaven and Earth.*

361 *Everything exists,*
is already,
in the seed.

362 You,
a sacred seed
were out there
in the void,
waiting,
to be born,
even before the birth of your parents.

363 All paths,
come,
from the void,
and,
return to the void

364 | *There is no death for the enlightened.*

365 | Each and every life, is, an unfinished dream.

Richard Kirsten Daiensai was born in Chicago and has been a resident of Seattle since 1940. He spends six months of every year living, studying, and painting in Japan and in 1967 he was ordained a Zen priest.

His vibrant works reflect personal transformations and embrace the essence of Tao, Zen, Shinto, and the divine energy that exists in all things. Daiensai studied at the Art Institute of Chicago and the University of Washington and his exquisite art appears in museums and collections throughout the United States and Asia, including the Library of Congress, Washington D.C.; First National Bank, Tokyo; the Metropolitan Museum of Art and Museum of Modern Art, New York; and the Seattle Art Museum, Seattle.